Gas Station Business

SMART Start-Up

How to Measure Profitability

How to Come up with a Valuation

How to calculate the ROI

How to Write the Best Business Plan

How to Get Financing

By

Shabbir Hossain

CSB Academy Publishing Co.
P. O. Box 966
Semmes, Alabama 36575, USA

Cover designed
By
Angela Jackson

First Edition

Table of Contents

Who Should NOT buy This Book

If you read my first book, "How to Start, Run and Grow a Gas Station Business" then I would suggest you not buy this book, as my first book does cover every topic including how to market and grow your business.

If you are a subscriber/listener of my podcast show, you should not buy this book either, as I have covered most of what I mention in this book in various episodes of my podcast show.

This book is truly a summary of a few episodes of my podcast show. You may ask why would I publish it as a book. Well, after writing the first book and starting my podcast, I have realized some people want fast and quick answers to 6 very common questions. They don't want to read a 200 page book that includes everything under the sun about a Gas Station Business.

In my first book, I talked a lot about how to find and buy the ideal business, then I went on to talk about how to grow that business with proper marketing and merchandising strategies. But in this book I simply answer the 6 most asked questions ever.

1. How do I find a good business for Sale?

2. How to find out how much money a gas station is making?

3. How do I come up with right pricing/valuation of a gas station?

4. What is The Return On Investment (ROI) in a gas station Business?

5. How to write the best business plan for a gas station.

6. How do I get a bank to finance my deal?

In last 3 years, these are the 6 questions I received over and over in my email, more than any other questions.

So this book is a quick start up guide for those who are looking to get into gas station business and need to find these answers in a hurry.

I also included a 15 step buying process checklist along with a 7 step closing checklist. This way you are covered start to finish in your buying process.

Lastly, after reading this book, if you think it was useful, I would love to see a review from you wherever you happen to pick up this book from(Amazon, iTunes, Kobo, etc.).

I promise to mention your name on my podcast show so I can properly say 'Thank You.'

About the Author

Shabbir Hossain graduated from the University of South Alabama in 1994 with a BS degree in Business Marketing. He started his first business the year before graduating – Byte 1 Computers and Software, where Shabbir and his friend and partner built and sold computers to various local businesses. In those days, the demands for personal computers were not very great, so they ended up closing the doors in just 18 months.

After moving to Tampa, Florida, Shabbir leased a BP gas station from a local company, launching his first gas station venture. Shortly after that, he applied to the BP Oil Corporation to become an authorized dealer and was ultimately selected to lease and operate either one of two stations. One was in Greenville, SC, and the other one in Mobile, AL.

Having lived in Mobile before, Shabbir chose to move back to Mobile and worked hard to build up a relationship with the local community there. Before long, Shabbir owned seven gas stations and secured yearly sales were over $5 million dollars on a consistent basis.

In last 20 plus years in business, he has owned, leased, operated and/or sold over 25 Gas Station Businesses. Along with gas stations, he also has been involved in many other retail businesses, like the Quiznos fast food chain, liquor stores, a Laundromat and even a wholesale operation where he sold to 85 local gas stations and convenience stores.

The key behind Shabbir's rapid success was mostly common sense marketing, creative promotion, and innovative new age merchandising skills – the type of strategies that so many gas station owners overlook, along with common sense location management strategies.

Today, Shabbir shares his knowledge and expertise of gas station business management via the CStore Business Academy blog site (http://gasstationbusiness101.com).

Shabbir recently started a new weekly audio podcast show called "Gas Station Business 101 Podcast". In this podcast he talks about all the recent changes, opportunities, and challenges of today's gas station business. He also shares tips, tricks and ideas on how to start, run and grow a gas station business successfully in today's economy.

You can find his show in many of the fine podcasting directories like iTunes, Stitcher, Blubrry, and Tunein radio.

Shabbir Hossain

C STORE BUSINESS ACADEMY

Gas Station Business SMART Start-UP

1. Why Should I Invest in a Gas Station Business?

Let's start from the very beginning and talk about some basics like what a gas station business is and why and how to get into one.

But first here are some facts about the gas station business. There are little over 151,000 gas stations and convenience stores in the US alone. Out of those 151,000, about 126,000 are selling fuel, so those are gas stations in a real sense. The rest are convenience stores without fuel.

The combined sales for all these 151,000 stores as of December 2013 were 700 billion with a B!! It is a pretty huge number!!! Almost 3/4 of a trillion dollars if you think about it, when the whole US GDP is only around 17 trillion.

Now that I have your attention, let's talk about the growth of this industry. Just in 2013, there were a little over 2000 new stores built across the US, again another big number. So, as you can see, it is a fast growing industry. More and more people are finding out about this recession proof business and jumping into the band wagon.

What is Gas Station Business?

A typical gas station has two main parts - Gasoline or fuel, and then there is the Convenience store where we sell from soda pop, candy, milk, and snack foods to tobacco and beer. Most typical convenience stores carry around 2000 items or SKU (Stock Keeping Unit); you can think of them as mini grocery stores, but with fuel.

If you are new to this, you may ask "why should I get into this line of business?" Well, the answer is simple, it is truly a recession-proof business, and, after 2008, every gas station business owner will agree that, even though the business slowed down during the depression era, it never went away.

Instead, the business came back stronger. Regardless if people have jobs or not, they still need fuel for their cars. If some of them are smokers, they still need their cigarettes as well as soda and candy for their kids. Well, you get the picture; we provide some of the very basic necessities to our community.

Another reason is that the risk of failing is much lower compared to most other retail businesses; again it goes back to what you are selling, and you are selling the basic necessities for our daily life.

Fuel for your car is neither a luxury, nor is the gallon of milk for your kids. Not every retail store sells basic necessities; think about a pizza shop, a beauty salon or a sporting goods store, none of which are considered basic necessities.

How Do I Get Started in a Gas Station Business?

Now that we have established it is a good line of business to get into, let's talk briefly about how to get into it.

It is a vast topic, and I will touch on some major points, but if you need more in-depth information, I would direct you to my blog which can be found at www.gasstationbsuiness101.com. You can also read my book How to Start, Run and Grow a Successful Gas Station Business. You can also join my

Facebook Group where we discuss everything about the business, and you can ask and get answers to questions you may have.

There are 3 ways to start or get into a gas station or convenience store business.

One way is to buy an existing business.

The second way is by leasing an existing business.

The 3rd way is where you build a new gas station and start that way, though if you are new to this business, I would strongly recommend you not try this 3rd option.

Depending on your budget, leasing is usually the most cost-effective way to get into this business; this is how I got started. Leasing also gives you greater flexibility to get out of it in the event that you decide this is not for you.

If you are in the market to buy such a business, there are few things you have to decide first.

What Brand of Gas Station Should I Buy?

If you want to buy a gas station, should you worry about what brand of fuel it carries? What brand should you buy and how important is branding? I get asked these questions quite often.

Even though the question sounds simple enough, the answer is not so simple. The best answer is 'it depends'. It depends on many factors such as your geographic location, the locality, the neighborhood that business is located in, and what the dominant brands in that area are.

Some brands are stronger in some cities and states than others. For example, BP brand has always been the strongest brand in Ohio, and one big reasons is that BP is based out of Cleveland,

Ohio. So if you are in Ohio, I would say that if you can start a BP branded store, you will have strong credit card base to support your business.

But if you are buying a Convenience store, than the most important factor is what neighborhood is that business located in. Typically convenience stores without fuel only thrive in densely populated inner city locations. But there are always exceptions to every rule, so just keep that in mind.

Getting into a business such as this takes a big long-term commitment. There is certainly a decision-making process we all go through, but most importantly the question you should ask yourself first is "am I cut out to do this?" Before you answer, find out what it take to be a successful gas station business owner.

Dedication, attention to detail, love for numbers, repeating the process and being a people person are what most successful business owners possess

If your answer is yes, then you are on your way to a good start to a better and brighter future for you and your family.

How Much Money Do I Need?

Next, let's talk money. A common question I get asked is "how much do I need to get into a gas station business?" The answer, once again, is 'it depends'. Well yes, it does. A gas station in NYC with real estate may cost you as high as 3-7 million dollars, when a similar type station may cost only 1.5 million in a small city in Alabama, Mississippi or Tennessee.

Same goes for leasing; it can be very high in some parts of the country while not so expensive in other parts. It all boils down to the basic economics of supply and demand. Where demand is high and supply is limited, the price will be higher.

On the other hand, leasing a similar store by itself can cost much less then when you buy it with real estate. So if you are on a limited budget, your goal would be to find a good station that is for lease.

A typical lease deal often requires that you pay for goodwill; goodwill is an amount you pay to the seller for the opportunity that he or she is transferring to you so you can make money from operating the business. On top of the goodwill money, you also have to pay for the entire inventory aka the merchandise that is in the store. There are some additional expenses such as security deposits, first month's rent and such.

 If you are wondering whether you can get a bank to finance your deal, then the answer is yes. Provided you have good credit, enough collateral, tax returns showing solid income for previous years along with good business plan then yes, there are plenty of loan options available out there.

 But do remember banks typically only finance when you buy with real estate and not a leased property, as there is nothing tangible for them to hold on to in the event you default.

Should I Lease or Buy a Gas Station Business?

Now let's talk about leasing vs. buying. If you are limited on funds, then leasing may be the option for you. But remember, it is hard to find a store to lease with no money down. Even if you find one, it may not be a good one. But leasing a good store often requires a little less cash than actually buying that same store with real estate.

 If you have access to credit (when I say access I mean you have good credit), great tax returns for last 3 years showing decent income and some down payment, my advice is you should try and buy something with real estate and not try the leasing option. There are quite a few benefits to doing that.

First, you are creating an asset. Well, yes, it is an asset that makes your net worth look higher than before. Not only that, but most commercial loans are typically anywhere from 7-15 years term, so in 15 years you pay off the loan and then you are sitting on a paid off income generating property that is making money for you every month.

Second, there are a few tax advantages to buying vs. leasing. You can get tax deduction for the interest you paid to your lender. Also all your equipment that came with the store including gasoline pumps, register, walk-in coolers, tanks, even the building and canopy can be depreciated in your accounting books for a certain number of years which is a big saving in actual dollars.

2. Where to Find a Business to Buy or Lease?

If you are new to Gas Station business but have enough interest to dig deeper into this business, then the next step for you is to try and find a few businesses for sale and evaluate them the best way possible and see if any of them fit your budget and needs.

As I mentioned before, a gas station business is truly a recession-proof business and still provides a comfortable living for a family. Not to mention the freedom it provides by having and owning your own business.

If you are serious about finding a suitable gas station business to buy or lease, there are many ways to find gas stations or convenience stores that are for sale in your area.

You can try both Online and Offline ways.

5 Offline Ways to Find a Business for Sale:

You can try:

1. Through Local business brokers (Some national and some local. Two of the major national brokerage companies are Sunbelt and Nationwide business brokers. Local or statewide would like Gas Station USA brokers in FL)

2. Through Local commercial real estate agents

3. Through Local newspaper classified

4. Through Local oil and fuel Jobbers/wholesaler

5. Through Vendors (this works only if you are already in this line of business)

5 Online Ways to Find a Business for Sale

There are some very reputable websites you can go and check for sale listings; then there are also online auction houses that sell gas stations among other businesses.

1. First, check out bizbuysell.com. This site is similar to realtor.com for home real estate, but in this site, business brokers list their businesses that are for sale.

2. Try searching on NRC.com. and Loopnet.com. Both of these are big players when it comes to online business brokerage. You will find both "for sale stores" and "for Lease stores."

3. Craigslist ads. Yes, you can find them under "business for sale."

4. Do a search for auction houses that sell commercial properties

5. You can also just do a google search by typing "gas station for sale in Los Angeles, Ca" Just mention your city and state and see what comes up.

But before you contact any of the sellers or brokers, you need to have your game plan set, so you don't sound like you are just browsing the market.

Business brokers are very different than typical home real estate agents. If a broker senses that you are not serious they may not even disclose some of their prime listings to you. The reason is simple; they don't want to take a buyer who is not serious to a seller who is motivated to sell. This can take away from the broker's credibility in front of the seller. Also, sellers typically only want serious and qualified buyers that are ready to buy.

You will notice that, before a broker discloses any information about a business, they will want you to sign a document called an NDA (Non-Disclosure Agreement). This is required because you are being exposed to some confidential and sensitive financial information about a business. Once you sign the NDA, you are in a contract that says you are not to disclose the information you are about to receive with just anyone.

Also, another thing to keep in mind when visiting any of the potential stores for sale, that most times the business owners do not want the employees to know that they are selling the business. Sometimes there is a good reason for it. So first sit down and figure out what your budget is, what your game plan is, and how soon you want to get into a business. Once you know these three, you are half way there.

Just remember when you contact a business broker, they may ask you a lot of questions to figure out what, exactly, you are looking for. They may ask about your budget; it is usually a good idea not to answer that with a dollar figure, instead tell them that it varies depending on what is out there. This way they will show you a wide range of businesses. Some may be over your budget, and some below, but this way you can see where the market stands. It gives you a baseline of the highs and the lows of your market.

Once you have a list of 3-4 businesses to look at it, that is when your real work starts. First, you need to visit all the locations so you have a visual feel for them. Take plenty of notes; best is to take notes where you write down the good the bad on each side so later you can see what the good points are and what the bad points are of a business and if the bad ones outweigh the good ones.

You can also use a marketing tool I often use called an MA-CP grid, where you draw a square box with 4 mini squares that are equal to the square in that big box and, on the left of this box, I write MA, which stands for market attractiveness and on the bottom I write CP or competitive positioning. I try to place each of the business in one of those squares based on their location, sales, nearest competitors, etc.

If a store has very high market attractiveness, you should place it on the high side of the quadrant. Similarly, if a store has a very good competitive position in the market, it should be placed at the "high" side as well. Ideally you want to pick the store/business that ranks high on both market attractiveness and competitive positioning. This way you know you are looking at a winner.

	High	Low
High	2	3
Low	1	4

Market attractiveness

Competitive position

Once you narrow down to, let's say, 2-3 stores out the 5, time to tell your broker or seller that you are interested in finding out more about their business.

If you have come this far, then you are well on your way to be a business owner soon. But before you say yes, remember, once you narrow down to a handful stores, time to do a thorough due diligence on each of your findings.

Once you do good and thorough work, the right one will come out of that bunch, and you will know which business is the right one for you to make an offer on.

3. How Do I Know if The Price is Right?

When doing a valuation of a gas station business, it is usually not as simple as doing a valuation of a home. The standard practice for a home appraisal is simple; You look at the following:

- SQF of the home

- build quality

- the structure of the home

- age of the home

- location of the home

Then compare these factors with nearby similar homes that were sold in last 12 months and you can come up with a general idea where the value should be

But when it comes to a gas station appraisal, it is not that easy, as there are two parts to a good valuation of any gas station business.

1. **The Real Estate Part**

2. **The Business Part**

The real estate part of the value can vary widely based on its geographic location

A corner lot with an acre of land can cost 3x-7x more in bigger cities like NY or Chicago compared to a small town in Kentucky or Alabama.

Now, the business part of the valuation also can depend on many factors, such as:

1. Fuel volumes

2. Number and type of fuel dispensers and related payment technology

3. Site location and visibility

4. Condition and age of the facility

5. Size of the building

6. Demographic and regional growth trends

7. Branded versus unbranded

8. Number and distance of competitors if big names retailers nearby or not

9. Traffic counts

10. Diversification of revenue streams

11. Ingress and egress

12. Profitability and trends

13. With or Without Deli/Restaurant or Car wash

There are ways you can still find a good valuation for a business that you are interested in buying.

My approach is to find out what the value is as listed in the local tax assessor's office; that is your county property tax office. They keep a valuation on every piece of real estate in your local county.

In most areas you can just go online to your local county tax commissioner's website and type in the address and find out what they are listing as the value of any property

Now, don't get excited when you see that value, as it is usually much less than actual market value, sometimes even less than half or even lower, but at least this way I find my base point of the pricing.

Then, if you are using a business broker or agent, ask them to find you a list of gas stations/c-stores that have sold in last two years in your area. Once you have that list with the selling prices, visit those stores.

Typically your brokers or agents can give you a list of those stores with selling price and sales data attached to them. This way you can do some calculation and find out which of those stores match closest to the business you are looking to buy.

Looking through these previously sold stores, you can figure out two things. First, the average selling price of a store based on sales numbers, and secondly, how much the market will bear in your area.

Remember, you have your base $ amount value from the tax commissioner's office, and now you have the asking price of businesses you are looking at and an average of a few previously sold similar businesses in your area. As long as you can stay in the middle of those two numbers, you are doing better than most.

Now let's talk about how to find a value of a leased business or a business that is for lease. How do you know what the value should be of that business? When I say value, I mean the goodwill amount.

There are plenty of theories floating around on this topic; some will tell you the selling price should be between 2 to 2.5 times the gross monthly merchandise sales of the store. Some will say three times the sales, but again doing some research through your local brokers can be very helpful. Ask them to show you some similar businesses that sold in your area recently and see if they are actually sold for similar value.

So, for example, if a store is doing $100,000 merchandise sales a month, not including fuel sales, then the value/price according to that formula would be 250k-300k for you to buy the lease of that business.

But let's say you found a business that is doing $100,000 in merchandise sales a month and the price was 230k to buy the lease, is that a good deal? Well, it depends on many factors like what the rent is, how much fuel it sells, what the actual gross profit margin of that merchandise sales is.

Now, if the rent is set at $10,000 a month, and if the gross profit margin is very low in the store, then at the end of the month after paying your rent, utility, payroll and all other expenses, you may lose money.

So you have to look at the whole picture and do some serious calculation first. Just remember; sales numbers only tell you half the story, the other half is what you have to find out on your own. No business brokers or agents will tell you that.

Then there is another method called the multiple method. In this method, they generally take the net earnings of a business and multiply that number by anywhere from 1-3, and that is the selling price. Let's say a business shows it made a net profit of $100,000 in 2014, the seller of that business can ask three times that earnings which would translate to $300,000.

If you find sellers that are using this method, then it is beneficial to ask and take a look at three years earnings vs. just one year. This way you get to see a trend, and not just a snapshot.

Now a little story time about my first gas station venture. I am sharing this to show you how asking price of a business sometimes has nothing to do with the earnings or even sales.

I mentioned this on my very first podcast episode. I bought my first gas station business in Tampa FL. At the time I didn't know anything about the gas station business. I saw an ad in the newspaper that said a gas station was for lease for a reasonable price. I went and visited the store; it looked big and bright, and I saw some traffic coming in and out. I figured it must be a great business.

The sellers were asking $45,000 plus the cost of inventory. They provided me last three months of sales data which showed the store was doing around $45,000 in merchandise sales and about 40,000 gallons of fuel. The deal in fuel was that I would get a commission only, which I think was around 6 cents on each gallon sold. The rent was set at $4,500/month and, according to the sellers, the store's average profit margin was 30%

I then sat down with a pen and paper and calculated the gross income for a month vs. gross expenses for the same month

So for merchandise gross profit, it would be 45k x 30% = $13,500

And for gasoline, I would make 40k gallon x 6 cents = $2400 every month

Now add those two and my total gross profit for a month would be $15,900

Then I looked at my expenses, and they were like this:

Rent $4500

Payroll $3500

Utility bills combined was $2500

So total expenses for a month would be $10,500

I was excited that I would be making around $5,000 a month. That would translate into $60,000 a year for me which was a huge $$$ number. I even thought if I cut down labor to just one employee and work myself about 8 hours every day then I could save even more.

So I borrowed some funds from friends and family and took cash advances from all 4 of my credit cards and gathered up $35,000. I went and asked the sellers if they would consider financing the remaining $5,000 along with the cost of inventory for 12 months. They readily agreed, and I bought my very first business.

Now here is the sad part. Even with a business degree, I failed to investigate a few minor but very valuable details. I failed to check the actual profit margin of the store.

In just two months What essentially started happening was a slow but steady death of my business due to lack of profit margin. I didn't have money in the bank; I was overdrawing my bank account. I was bouncing checks even with the utility companies.

I let 2 of the 3 employees go and started working myself from open to close 18 hours a day. I would only bring in one employee for 3 hours each day. I still remember Lorrie my very first employee, a very sweet and honest lady. I had her come and work for 3 hours every day while I went and took care of bank deposits, picked up store supplies from Sam's Club, took a shower and picked up food for myself.

Since I knew I was the only one working for the most part, it was not theft that was causing my negative cash flow. I figured it had to be the lack of profit margin.

I then sat down and started analyzing my profit margin for each item I sold in my store. I Found out I was working on very low margin. For example, in cigarettes I was only making 7% profit, while on beer and wine I was doing 12% and the rest was only around 18-20%.

I figured out the game the sellers played with me. They bought stores that didn't do very well; they lowered all the prices much below the competitors to built up the business. Once the sales went over $40,000, they sold the business for a profit.

After much calculation, I figured out my average gross profit was only 16.5% and not 30% like the sellers said.

In reality, I was bringing in 45,000 x 16.5% = $7425 from merchandise sales, and $2400 from fuel commission.

Adding the two gross profit 7425 + 2400 = $9825 which is less than the monthly expenses of $10,500. Not to mention I was making a monthly note payment of $2800 to the sellers to pay off the balance they financed. I was losing little over $3,500 each month.

I had no other choice but to raise prices. I did it slowly, one item at a time and in 9 months I went from combined gross profit of 16. 5% to around 28%. Luckily I didn't lose many sales. Once the business became profitable, I sold it and moved on.

That was a very tough chapter in my life, but it did teach me some very valuable lessons about this line of business and I am glad and thankful to the sellers for me putting me through that learning curve. It was hard, I will admit, but as I said, that lesson became very helpful later in my business life.

Now, coming back to the point of leasing or buying a business with high sales figures, as you can see, those numbers don't mean a whole lot until you check the actual profit margin of the business.

Remember, if you find a deal or offer too good to be true, then it probably is.

4. How Much Money Can I Make a Month?

I get asked this question a whole lot: "How much can I make from operating a gas station?"

Well, once again the answer is - it depends.

Yes, it does depend, on many factors like:

- Your monthly sales both of merchandise and fuel

- Your COGS (Cost of Goods Sold)

- Your total monthly expenses.

For example, you can have a store selling $100,000/month sales in merchandise making $5,000 a month vs. another store doing $70,000/month and making $8,000 each month.

You ask how?

Well, the 100k selling store may have higher expenses, and lower profit margin compared to the 70k selling store. So, yes, it depends on all those factors.

Every store is unique, and just learning the sales figure does not tell you the whole story. You always have to look at the whole picture to understand if any of them are profitable or not.

Then again, you may find a store that has high sales volume and good profit margin, but it is not making money. It could be because of some other reasons like theft, being mismanaged, by the recklessness of the owner or by unnecessarily high payroll numbers, or it could be a number of other reasons most of which can be rectified with little work.

I have taken over stores many times where the numbers did show a loss, but I did go through the deal because I knew what was wrong and knew how to fix it.

In this type of situation, you have to have some experience under your belt. But the task is doable as long as you can properly identify the issues that are causing the business not to show a profit.

Here are two P&L statements of a store (A true example I shared on podcast episode 23 and again on 29). In the first one, you will see how it was operating at a loss. Then look at the 2nd one. This one was prepared 4 months after the new owners came in and made a few improvements. You will see how the sales went up slightly, but the business started to show a much bigger profit numbers.

If you look carefully, you will notice that the fuel sales pretty much remained identical, but the merchandise sales went up by about $14,000. The store went from losing $2,500 to making little over $5,000, a jump of about $7,500.

This amazing change in profitability was the direct result of a few operational changes, and some serious marketing efforts undertaken by the sellers. I feel proud of their effort. I was hired to consult the buyers; I also drew the whole marketing plan which was a true success.

Once again, just because a store has high sales doesn't mean it is making good money or vice versa. You have to look at the whole picture, do some calculation, and see where each store stands on profitability (I know I am repeating myself here again, but I wanted to make sure you understand how important this truly is).

Typically a neighborhood gas station business with average sales should make anywhere from $5,000/month on the low end to about $15,000/month on the high end. But again, do remember there are exceptions to every rule.

Subject Store 1 Actual
Profit and Loss Statement
Oct-15

Store Revenue:

Fuel Sales(G)		$78,817.59	
Fuel COGS		$72,418.52	
Fuel Profit			$6,399.07
C-Store sales		$52,186.25	
C-Store COGS		$39,329.41	
C-Store Profit			$12,856.84
Other Income			
	Vaccume/Air	$214.52	
	ATM	$527.00	
Total O. Income			$741.52
Gross Profit:			**$19,997.43**

Store Expenses:

Payroll	$6,072.00	
Utility	$2,501.69	
Rent	$7,500.00	
T&I	$1,000.00	
C.C. Charge	$4,221.00	
Maintenance	$369.25	
License &Mics	$375.00	
Shortage & loss	$250.00	
Supplies	$283.00	
Total Expense		**$22,571.94**
Net Profit(Loss):		**($2,574.51)**

Subject Store 1
Profit and Loss Statement
Mar-16

Store Revenue:

Fuel Sales(G)		$79,701.30	
Fuel COGS		$70,619.99	
Fuel Profit			$9,081.31
C-Store sales		$66,466.03	
C-Store COGS		$49,234.53	
C-Store Profit			$17,231.50
Other Income			
	Vaccume/Air	$375.50	
	ATM	$611.45	
Total O. Income			$986.95

Gross Profit: | | | $27,299.76
Store Expenses:

Payroll	$6,529.84	
Utility	$2,141.08	
Rent	$7,500.00	
T&I	$1,000.00	
C.C. Charge	$4,497.62	
Maintenance	$179.62	
License &Mics	$81.77	
Shortage & loss	$100.00	
Supplies	$76.50	
Total Expense		$22,106.43

Net Profit: | | $5,193.33

5. How Can I Tell if A Business is Making Money?

Let's now talk about a real life example and some basic calculations to figure out if a business for sale makes money or not.

I recently came across a station for sale by an oil company; they gave me some sales volume for the last three years.

In 2015 their average monthly merchandise sales were $37,000. Monthly average fuel sales were 63000 gallons. All other monthly income averages were $860 (ATM, Air, Vacuum, etc.) monthly.

Let's first figure out their gross profit for each month. At 37k/Month Sale with 26% profit margins, their gross profit is $37,000 X 0.26 = $9620

On fuel, I noticed they average around 7-9 cents on Regular grade, 12-15 cents on Mid grade and around 20-25 cents on Premium grade fuel. I asked for a breakdown of their fuel sales, and this is how the calculation looked:

Average monthly regular gallon sold = 54,000 X .07 (cents) = $3,780

Average monthly Plus gallon sold = 4,000 X .12 (cents) = $480

Average monthly Premium gallon sold = 5,000 X .20(cents) = $1,000

So monthly fuel gross profit is $5,260

Let's now add fuel, merchandise and all other profit. $9,620 + $5,260 + $860 = $15,740

The next step is to figure out their monthly expenses:

I calculated the mortgage/rent to be $3,500 (The price is $350,000). In any of these type of investments it is safe to calculate the rent to be 1% of the total investment

Next, average payroll is $5,000 (the store is open 18 hours a day 365 days a year, single employee coverage so the math looks like this: 18 X30 (Days) X 9 ($9/hour which includes payroll taxes) =$4,860. I just rounded it off to $5,000 (but there is no management salary in this payroll).

Next, all utility bills together are around $2,750

Tax and insurance are right at $975

Credit card fees are around $2,450

Then I added all the rest, like license fees, shortage and loss, store supplies and maintenance. All of these items together came to $1,116

I know I am mentioning a lot of numbers, which can be confusing, but look at this below and it will make better sense.

Okay adding up all these expenses the total is $15,791

Now let's subtract the expenses from the gross profit so we can get to the net monthly profit dollar

$15,740 - $15,791 = ($51)

As you can see, the store is little short from reaching its break-even point.

Mini Mart For Sale
Profit and Loss Statement
2015 Average Monthly

Store Revenue:

Fuel Sales(G)	63,000.00	
Fuel COGS	57,740.00	
Fuel Profit		$5,260.00
C-Store sales	37,000.00	
C-Store COGS	27,380.00	
C-Store Profit		$9,620.00
Other Income		
Vaccume/Air	225.00	
ATM	635.00	
Total O. Income		$860.00

Gross Profit: $15,740.00

Store Expenses:

Payroll	5,000.00	
Utility	2,750.00	
Rent	3,500.00	
T&I	975.00	
C.C. Charge	2,450.00	
Maintenance	350.00	
License &Mics	366.00	
Shortage & loss	200.00	
Supplies	200.00	
Total Expense		**$15,791.00**

Net Profit (Loss) -$51.00

Now, if I were new to this business with limited funds and willing to work 10-12 hour days behind the counter, I would definitely buy this store.

Because I know by working the store I can build up the business and make it profitable. For people who will run with hired help, this is not a business they should buy.

I politely notified the sellers that I would not be moving forward with this store.

6. What is The ROI in a Gas Station Business?

Let's talk about ROI or Return On Investment. Typically, if you are leasing a business where there is not real estate involved, your investment should come back within the first 3-4 years. I have seen stores that returned the investments in just two years.

Say you leased a running gas station business for $200,000, and your monthly net profit is $8,500. In this case, you get your investment back in a little less than two years. But remember not to include the cost of inventory in this calculation, as it is considered an asset and not an investment for the long term.

Here is an example of a gas station for sale in our area. I saw an ad recently for a gas station that was for lease, I checked into it and found out it was legitimate. The owner asked for $195,000 Goodwill plus inventory at cost. The sales volume were: Inside merchandise $87,000-$115,000 monthly, Fuel 25k Gallons-30k Gallons monthly (sales varied from summer months to winter months). The rent they listed was $4500.

In my opinion, it was a great store to buy. See, the numbers have to justify the sales volume. In this scenario, I believe the goodwill that you will pay to buy this store will come back in little over 2 years, provided you operate the store properly and maintain the profit margin.

I did a quick P&L on this store based on the numbers and noticed the net profit is around $8,000, so for you to get your ROI back, take the goodwill amount only and divide that by the monthly net profit. 195,000/8,000 = 24.37 or roughly 24 and half months. So as you can see in this case, you will get your money back in just two years. This was a good investment.

Anytime you can get your initial investment back in 2-3 years; I say you are doing well.

Typically, if you buy a business with real estate, your monthly note payments are lower than if you actually leased that same store. This is how it works usually:

Let's say a gas station is valued at $800,000. If you lease that store, your typical rent will be at 1% of the total investment cost, which is $8,000/month, then you have to pay for T&I (Tax & Insurance)

On the other hand, if you bought that same with 20% down, at 6% APR financed for 15 years, your typical note payment will be around $5400 plus T&I. Not to mention all the tax benefits (interest deduction, depreciation) you get from buying, which adds to your bottom line at the end of each tax year.

As you can see, there is about $3,000 difference in just monthly payments, not to mention that if you lease that same property, you might have paid $100,000 goodwill just to get into it.

Where, if you buy the property, whatever down payment you pay comes off the total price of the property, so you are gaining instant equity on the business property.

Again, not to mention all the other benefits that comes from buying anything with real estate.

You will also get to write off the depreciation cost on equipment, fixtures and building every year, which will give you a nice tax savings every year.

7. How Can I Get Financing?

First, come up with a list of banks you want to apply to. It is not a good idea to apply at multiple banks at once. Instead, come up with a list of say, four banks, go and talk in depth with their business loan department and find out their full requirements.

In my experience, I have noticed typically smaller local banks are more inclined to offer loans to local gas stations than some of the bigger banks. But that may not be true for every part of the country, so it is best to talk to at least 3-4 banks and try to get the feel if they are really into this sort of business financing or not before you submit your application.

Sometimes your local business brokers or commercial real estate agents can guide you to the right bank, as they often deal with similar situations and know which banks are more favorable to these sort of loans. You can also ask your bank that you deal with every day and ask their advice.

Once you narrow down to 2 banks, make trips to meet their loan officer and see what their requirements are. Just remember, every bank will have similar requirements, but they can still vary widely based on many factors, like how much down payment they require and how much collateral they need from you, even if they offer some SBA assisted loans or not. Your goal would be to deal with a bank that offers SBA loans. SBA stands for Small Business Administration. SBA is a federal government agency whose primary goal is help small business owners get financing.

Most times the SBA offers some sort of guarantee (50-80%) on your behalf to the bank, so banks are somewhat more lenient in approving the loan as they are not in the risk for the total amount they are giving you. But the downside to this is the amount of paperwork you have to furnish is monumental in most cases.

The SBA's requirements can be broad and extensive, so be prepared to gather up a lot of paperwork.

Another drawback to an SBA loan, is it can take up to 6 months to get approval from them. They run slower than most banks and, in their defense, they do have a lot of applicants that are submitting applications, so they have to go through all that, and it is always first come first served, so be patient.

But if you have a larger down payment (say 30% or higher) or have some good collateral to offer then you can opt out on SBA loans and get most any banks to offer you a conventional loan. Provided you have all your ducks in a row, like your credit is in excellent shape, your tax returns show good incomes for previous years and so on so forth.

When you talk to any banks, they will hand you something called a loan package. Most times the package will have a checklist of documents that they want you to furnish to them along with a loan application and some other waiver forms, depending on your bank.

One thing to keep in mind: all banks and commercial lenders do have to follow certain guidelines that are set by federal and state banking authorities. Also, every bank will look at something called the LTV (Loan to Value) ratio of the property or business you are looking to buy. LTV is essentially where banks look at the actual value of the business you are looking to buy and how much of that value they can loan you.

But in any case, let's look at the list of documents you will need to get ready to submit to your bank. Some of these items I will mention here may not be on your bank's checklist, but do gather them anyway as it will make you look more professional and business like.

First the items you will need from the seller for this loan process:

- Last two years of P&L

- Last three years Tax Returns of the business

- A balance sheet

- Any and all inspection documents of the UST (Underground Storage Tanks)

Now here is what you need to gather:

1. You need to get copies of at least last 3 years of tax returns. Make sure the copies are signed.

2. Your resume (they may not even ask you for it, but remember the person that may approve your loan may never meet you but this way at least he or she gets to see who you are and how qualified you are. It always helps)

3. Copy of your Corp. Articles, (yes, you have to get this done before you even apply for your loan. I will touch on how to file a corporation in the next chapter).

4. Personal financial statement for all Corp. Officers or members (explain). Make sure to sign it. If you are married and file joint tax returns, than your wife needs to have one prepared for her as well, or you can make a joint personal financial statement for both of you and make sure to both sign that document.

5. Copy of the commercial appraisal

6. Copy of signed purchase agreement and Letter of Intent

7. Copy of your EIN (Employer's Identification Number) issued by the IRS

8. Copy of all member/partner's Driver's licenses and social security cards

9. A well thought out and expertly written Business Plan (not a store bought one or copy-pasted one; one that is written for that specific business. Get help if you need to, but this has to be a well thought out plan. Do it like your life depends on it. Trust me on this.) Listen to my podcast episode # 27, where I broke down the entire process of what to include in your business plan. You can also go to My Blog and take a look at a sample business plan that I used for a business loan.

10. Last but not least, the loan application all filled out. Use a computer and printer if possible. If not, write very clearly, so it is easy to read.

11. A cover letter addressed to the loan Dept. where you describe what is in the package and thanking them for reviewing your loan application. Lastly, tell them where they can find you if they need further help or additional documents from you. It just makes you look more professional

Now remember to organize these papers with nice tabs and in a binding folder where anyone can open the folder, look at the tab and go directly to that specific section.

Just remember, based on the age of the facility you are looking to buy, banks may also ask for some environmental tests done on the health status of your UST. These tests are often known as Phase I test and Phase II tests. What these tests are designed to do is find out if they are any leaks or corrosion in the tanks, how solid they are, and if any of them leaked previously. In the event they want any of these tests done, you have to hire a local professional fuel equipment servicing company to do that. If I recall, a Phase I test usually cost around $1,000, and Phase II usually costs around $3,000-$5,000 depending on where you are.

If you are applying for an SBA-specific business loan, then SBA may also give you a loan package with some more documents and forms to fill out.

Now let's talk about business plan in little more in depth

A typical business plan starts with something called an executive summary where you introduce yourself (and your partners if you have any). In a short paragraph, summarize what you are planning to do and how you plan to be successful. This way, your readers will get an idea where this business plan is leading to before reading through the whole document.

Next, you will talk about the company you formed that you want to buy this business under, explain who is in this company and how many shares they each have, what their roles are in the company and who the person in charge will be.

Next, you will talk about the management team, who will be in this team, and what their roles are.

Next, you will talk about products and services your new business will offer or sell. Remember, the person reading your business plan may not be a pro when it comes to a gas station business, so you have to really explain how you will be conducting your gas station business.

Next, you need to draw a picture with words and explain who your competitors are, and how they may affect or benefit you.

Now you need to focus on who your target market is and explain your customer base. Again, keep in mind that the person reading the plan may not know much about your business, so you need to explain who your target market is. It is a good idea to gather up some Census data and add here, for instance, what the population of your city is, data about demographics and income level and such.

Now comes the juicy part, marketing:

You need to explain in depth how you plan to market your store.

One of the best ways you can give your readers a snapshot of the business is by using this grid below and by mentioning what number represents your business in the market.

But before you do that, first let me explain what market attractiveness is. It is the way you can measure the potential value of your market. Here is a list of 6 items can you analyze to figure out how attractive the market is for your business:

1. Growth rate of the market

2. Size of the market

3. Competition in the market

4. short-term profitability of the market

5. Long-term Profitability of the market

6. Cost to enter the market

Once you carefully analyze these 6 items, then you can determine if your specific market is attractive to enter or not. Chances are that if you are writing a business plan for a specific business or a store, that means you have already made the decision to buy that business, and the market attractiveness of that business is HIGH.

Now as for the competitive positioning of your business you need to analyze these following 7 factors first:

1. Size of your market.

2. Identify your Immediate competitors.

3. What are the threats that you are facing in the market?

4. What are the strengths of your business in the market?

5. What are the weaknesses in the market?

6. Are there any opportunities in the market?

7. What is your unique selling proposition (USP)?

Once again, analyze these factors. First, look at your market as a whole, determine the size, and identify your direct competitors. But while doing so, remember to look at the strength vs. weakness and then opportunity vs. threats of the market, so you can better position yourself in the market. Lastly, identify your USP or unique selling proposition. This is where you come up with a set of values and attributes of your business that makes your business unique and stand out in the crowd.

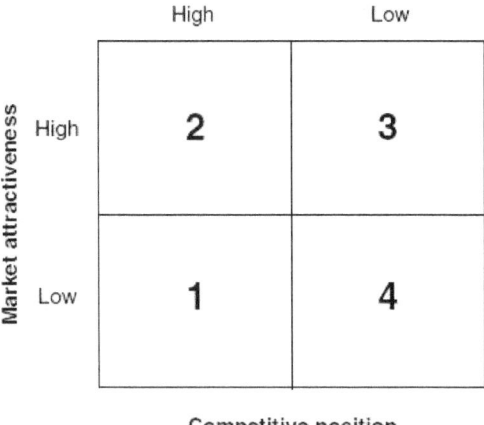

Once you explained and identified your MA vs. CP on that grid, it's time to come up a creative marketing plan.

You have to be specific and outline at least 2-3 good solid marketing strategies for your business. For example, you can say you will do 2000 direct mail outs to your local neighborhood and offer them a free hot dog when they buy a large soda, or you will have a banner advertising 99 cents for a 2-liter soda. You can also mention strategies like sponsoring the local kids basketball team or offering the local church free drinks for their Sunday service once a month.

I am sure you get the idea. Use bullet points to emphasize each marketing strategy.

In this segment, you can briefly talk about your creative pricing strategy, too. You can break it down into categories and show how, by adjusting some prices, you can have a positive impact on your business. Mention how you will offer lower prices compared to your competitor and how that can increase your revenue in business while still maintaining a good healthy profit margin

Financial plan (very important part that bank looks at).

In this segment of the business plan, you need to create some sales forecasts. You do not need to show how much profit you are making, but how much you will grow your sales over the next 3 years. If you need to see an example, visit my blog and you will find a sample business plan under "Resources."

Next, you can talk about your staffing plan. How many people will work in the business, and what will your payroll expenses be? In this section, you can even do a projected labor budget for next 3 years as you did for sales. Again, you can look at the example on my blog, or you can even download it.

Lastly, you need to add 3 years of projected P&L and make sure it is realistic. Best practice is to base your P&L on the P&L you get from your sellers. This way, they will look more realistic, but make sure it reflects the improvements you suggested you would do to the business, and the growth that you talked about.

8. Complete Gas Station Business Buying Process

Let's dive into the list and I will explain each and every process as we go forward.

1. Finding a Gas Station Business and doing the Due Diligence

The first step, I am sure you guessed, is that you have to have a business that you want to buy, right? So first, find a business you like, then do your due diligence and know the numbers and figure out if it is the right one for you. Once you do that you are half way there.

Now for the other half, you need to go few more steps before it is all said and done.

2. Valuation

As I mentioned earlier, valuation is a very key factor when buying any business, so follow the steps I outlined and hopefully you have the right valuation.

3. Letter of Intent

Letter of Intent is a preliminary offer letter from a buyer to a seller expressing your intent to buy the business for a certain price. This letter usually gets the ball rolling, so to speak.

4. Hire a Commercial Appraiser

If you are buying a business with the real estate included, and looking to get financing from a bank, you will need a commercial appraisal done first. But don't just hire anyone. Wait for the bank to tell you who they recommend, as every bank has their own preference as to whose appraisal they like.

5. Price Negotiation

Now is the time to negotiate the price with the seller.

Remember, your goal is to lower the asking price, and the seller's goal is stay closer to the asking price, so two things take place in a typical negotiation table. One, a smart buyer will point out all the negatives and shortcomings of that business while the seller will try to make you believe that there is nothing wrong with their business, and this is a deal of the century.

But before you go to the negotiating table, you need to find out how much your appraisal came back for. It is an important document for you and your loan application process. This is what the banks rely on heavily when it comes to approving your loan for a certain amount; that amount depends on this appraisal. Typically banks may say we can offer a loan 80% of the appraised value of the business.

From step two, you also know the valuation number you found by doing your research, so you should be well informed by now on the valuation.

It is a good idea to go to the negotiation table all prepared. First, you have to look hard at all the numbers the sellers gave you, such as the P&L, the balance sheet, etc. Then look at the notes you took when you first went to see the business location and come up with a list of negative items that you noticed about the business, and write them down.

And they could be items like:

Restrooms need an upgrade.

Sales floor has broken tiles, so you will have to redo the whole floor (which you may not do instead you may just fix the broken ones).

If it is an older facility, mention that the building needs to be painted.

If the fuel dispensers look a little dated, mention that you will have to spend money to upgrade the dispensers soon.

It is best not to mention 15--20 items but mention 2-5 items that you think need work, and then come up with a dollar value for those repairs or upgrades, and make sure the price you are offering reflects that. What I mean by that is:

Let's say the seller is asking 770k for the business, and you know the appraised value of the business is right at 735K. Now your goal is to go below that appraised value number. The lower you can go from that number the better off you are. Let's say you offer 670K. With that offer you can now also explain to the seller why it is lower than his or her asking price.

The reasons you can give are:

Number one, their asking price is higher than the appraisal value of the business.

Two, the 5 repair items that you mentioned to sellers before will cost around 65K, so what you did here is you took the appraisal value of the business and deducted the estimated repair cost, and that is how got that magic number of 670K.

Often times the sellers will strongly disagree. In my experience, some even disagree with the appraisal value, but in most cities there are only a handful of these commercial real estate and business appraisers that are approved by most lenders, so it is hard to argue with their valuation

Some sellers use tactics like "we have other offers". When you hear that, politely remind them every buyer has to go through this appraisal process and this the value they all will get, and that banks will never loan more than what the property has appraised for.

You may end up going up 10-15K higher on your original offer and may be able to seal the deal at around 685k. If you can do that you are a winner.

6. Signing a Purchase Agreement

Since you both agreed on the price and terms, time for you to sign a purchase agreement and put up some earnest money as a deposit, so the seller knows you are a serious buyer.

7. Loan Application

Time for you to go to a local bank and apply for a commercial loan. There are many different options available when it comes to commercial loans. It is best to ask a loan officer what type of loans are available out there, so don't forget to inquire about SBA (Small Business Administration) loans. These types of loans are typically designed by the federal government to help new small business owners get started.

8. Incorporating Your Business Entity

Here, if you have to decide what and how you want to structure your company, it is best to get some legal advice from an attorney that is knowledgeable about the business law. Often times, you will see that it is well worth the investment to pay an attorney to draw up your articles of organization, especially if you have more than one partner or member in your entity. If you have more than one business partner, then you may also ask your attorney to draw up a partnership agreement along with the articles of incorporation.

There are basically 3 types of company you can file for; one is S Corp., One is C Corp., and the 3rd is LLC or LLP

I am not an attorney, so I can't advise you on which entity will be best suited for your needs, but I can tell you what I have. I have a couple of LLC's and one S Corp. It is often a good idea to ask an attorney to file your legal entity for you.

9. Apply for EIN Number

While waiting for the bank loan to get approved, you can get a couple of things done in the meantime. Apply for an EIN number. If you have an accountant or a CPA ask them to apply on your behalf. An EIN number is essentially the social security number for your business. This is how the IRS identifies your business, as they identify you with your social security number.

10. Setting up the Closing Date

Once you hear from the bank that your loan is done, it is time to notify the seller and set up a closing date and time. In this meeting you need to discuss how you want to handle the transfer of inventory, and how to count and pay for them.

Best practice is to hire a company that counts inventory, this way you get a real exact 3rd party count and know what you are paying for.

Also, you both have to agree how to calculate the cost of that inventory. Remember, everything in the store is priced at retail, so you have to come up with the actual cost of that inventory. If not, you will pay too much.

There are many ways to do it, but some of the more common approaches are:

Get a total dollar figure of all merchandise and then take off 25-30% from the top and pay that, recalling the categories I talked about before and how much profit margin there was on each.

Well, some sellers do not want to go through each category and calculate each at a different percentage, they want to do it in one lump-sum, and that is fine, as long as you know you are not over or under paying for the inventory.

Some others offer cigarettes, beer and wine at actual cost and the rest at 30%. Again, it depends on the store and their selling prices and how much inventory they have. Each scenario is different, so you have to figure that out before agreeing to any deals.

But one very important thing to remember; when doing the inventory, make sure to tell the company that is doing your counting to check for outdated and/or expired products, so they can keep those products aside and not include them in their count. You should not pay for expired, damaged or out of date products.

11. Setting up Business Bank Account

Time to open a business bank account and order checks and deposit slips. One mini advice on that; make sure to order deposit slips that have a duplicate copy, it will help you a lot down the road.

12. Setting up Payroll Service

Talk to your accountant and figure out how to handle employee payroll.

13. Applying for Business Licenses

Ask the sellers about all the required licenses you have to apply for; there are some licenses that in some cities and states you have to apply for in advance.

 Get a list of all the licenses you need to apply for. Remember, in most cities, you will need a license from the city, the county, and the state. It is a good idea to go ahead and apply for the reseller's Tax id or sales tax license as you will need it from the very first day.

14. Meet the Employees

I usually meet the employees a day before closing, and let them know what is going on and assure them that their jobs are safe. Then I hand them each a new hire package with a job application and a w2, along with a checklist of job duties and responsibilities. I also hand each an acknowledgment letter that states everyone is on probation for the first 90 days so I can review their work performance. I have everyone sign that document. Some of the employees can be a little shaky, as they have a fear that you may fire them all and bring your own family to work, so try to put them at ease, but this is also the time to explain what is expected of them.

I always mention 2 things I look for in an employee; honesty and great customer service. These two are my topmost priority when it comes to employees. I also let them know that I do prosecute if I find anyone stealing from me.

15. The Actual Closing

Typically, a closing takes place at a title company or even at a bank; again it will depend on your bank. But in either case, this is when you and the seller meet and sign all the documents and the seller gets paid their money. I try to go and get the inventory counting part done before heading to the closing. This way I can pay the seller for the merchandise at the closing table.

If that doesn't work, then you can sign the closing papers at the bank, then go back to the store and do the inventory and write them a separate check for it.

Last but not the least, show up bright and early and be ready to work long hours the first few days of taking over a new business, as you need to learn so much of the new business.

Okay now let's recap so you can see it at a glance:

1. Finding a gas station business and doing the due diligence.

2. Valuation.

3, Letter of Intent.

4. Hire a commercial appraiser for an appraisal.

5. Price negotiation.

6. Signing a purchase agreement.

7. Loan application.

8. File your corporation.

9. Apply for EIN number.

10. Setting up the closing date.

11. Setting up Business Bank Account.

12. Setting up Payroll service.

13. Applying for Business License.

14. Meet the employees.

15. The Actual closing.

9. Closing Checklist

7 step closing checklist you must check off before you buying a Gas Station Business

I came up with a checklist so anyone can just write them down and make sure to check each and every item before signing off on a deal. You can apply to this to most any retail business purchase and save money.

Assuming you found the business that you like and negotiated a price and set up a closing date for you to take over. The day of the closing, typically, an inventory management company comes in that you hired and counts the entire retail inventory and gives you the report along with a dollar total of all inventory at cost. You pay the seller the cost of that inventory, and you are in business.

There are many moving parts to a business closing process that you need to be aware of. If done wrong they can cost you thousands of dollars, but following this 7 step checklist can save you thousands, so please do pay attention.

7 Step Closing Checklist

1. Check the merchandise pricing to make sure they are not out or range.

2. Negotiate the retail to cost percentage of the inventory you will be paying to the seller.

3. Plan with seller for transfer of all regulatory licenses.

4. Transferring all utilities under your company name.

5. Notifying all vendors about the change.

6. Identifying all unsalable merchandise at the closing day.

7. Follow proper Inventory counting process.

10. My Last Words

If you follow the steps I outlined in this book, you will be able to eliminate a lot of the risks associated with buying a new business. Just remember, if something seems too good to be true, then it probably is. So use common sense and don't let your guard down.

For more detailed information, you can listen to my weekly podcast Gas Station Business 101 Podcast on iTunes, Stitcher or TuneIn radio. You can also subscribe to my Newsletter where I share many valuable tools and tricks of the trade. It is all free, and I will not try to sell you anything, that's a promise.

If you have any questions, please feel free to send me an email at shabbir@GasStationBusiness101.com

Good luck!

www.ingramcontent.com/pod-product-compliance
Lightning Source LLC
Chambersburg PA
CBHW070406190526
45169CB00003B/1133